BOTTOM LINES

LIFE'S GOLDEN RULES™

BOTTOM LINES

The Golden Rules for Executive Success

GENERAL PUBLISHING GROUP
Los Angeles

The Life's Golden Rules series is published by General Publishing Group, Inc, 3100 Airport
Avenue, Santa Monica, CA 90405, 310-915-9000.

Library Catalog Number 93-79388
ISBN 1-881649-12-1

10 9 8 7 6 5 4 3 2 1

Quay Hays, Editor
Design by Deborah Daly
Conceived by Stan Corwin
PRINTED IN THE USA

To

Paris and Mason

LEARN

HAVE FUN

PROSPER

BOTTOM LINES

1 ❖ Have at least one original idea a day.

2 ❖ Never accept responsibility without authority.

3 ❖ Know when to phone instead of fax.

4 ❖ Spend only as you get.

5 ❖ Thank someone for a job well done.

6 ❖ No one can make you feel inferior without your consent.

7 ❖ Power is only in the hands of those you give it to.

8 ❖ Give to one homeless person on your way to
work. If you can't afford it, stop long enough
to wish them luck.

9 ❖ Read *Getting to Yes*.

10 ❖ Keep in touch with your old company.

11 ❖ Never assume.

12 ❖ Control the pace. Pacing is everything.

13 ❖ Hire away from your hang-ups.

14 ❖ Keep a card on you that has your phone
     number, car phone number, fax number,
     Federal ID number, resale number and car
     fax number.

15 ❖ Don't be an assistant to anybody with whom you don't get along.

16 ❖ In all good business deals, what makes the best business sense is to follow the money.

17 ❖ Inside every problem are the seeds of a solution.

18 ❖ Don't con other people.

19 ❖ Don't con yourself.

20 ❖ Reluctance feeds the aggressor.

21 ❖ Keep your word.

22 ❖ Be a part of the solution, not the problem.

23 ❖ Try not to give ultimatums.

24 ❖ Pay the IRS on time. Late taxes can be your
worst nightmare.

25 ❖ Learn the art of schmoozing but don't make
it your greatest talent.

26 ❖ Leave the Christmas party early—you'll be glad when you hear the stories the next day.

27 ❖ The best leader is not the one who makes the fewest mistakes, but the one who makes the best of them.

28 ❖ "People who want simple solutions are mediocre. The ability to endure with problems is the secret of greatness."—*Armand Erpf*

29 ❖ Find a mentor.

30 ❖ Mentor somebody.

31 ❖ Spend a few minutes reading
   The 1 MinuteManager.

32 ❖ Cut out one meeting a day.

33 ❖ Keep a paper trail of your actions and decisions.

34 ❖ Mail the originals of what you fax.

35 ❖ Hire a consultant only if you can't do it.

36 ❖ Remember the oldest adage—an honest
   day's pay for an honest day's work.

37 ❖ Take pride in your work and your
   reputation.

38 ❖ Learn from your last deal.

39 ❖ Overcome shyness.

40 ❖ When explaining, eschew obfuscation and
  prolixity.

41 ❖ Time is precious. Start at the end and say it
  in two minutes or less.

42 ❖ Use your own product and see if it works.

43 ❖ Don't work for a company that doesn't have a conscience.

44 ❖ Read your company's annual report.

45 ❖ Never skimp when it comes to attorneys and accountants.

46 ❖ He who is his own lawyer has a fool for a client.

47 ❖ Find yourself a personal banker and get acquainted.

48 ❖ Limit the weekly meeting to one hour.

49 ❖ Do a P and L forecast for your business and
for your life.

50 ❖ "Winning is the only thing."

—Vince Lombardi

51 ❖ For every business lunch you have,
   have lunch with a friend or co-worker.

52 ❖ Don't pad your expense account.

53 ❖ Walk to lunch when possible.

54 ❖ When possible, grow with equity, not debt.

55 ❖ Stay in touch with your alma mater and your old hometown.

56 ❖ Be kind to people on the way up—you will most certainly meet them again.

57 ❖ Tell the boss you'd like his/her job
someday, but only if you mean it.

58 ❖ Go through your rolodex at least once a
month to update and discard.

59 ❖ Then call somebody you haven't talked to
in a while.

60 ❖ There's nothing wrong with nepotism.

61 ❖ Know someone at your parent company.

62 ❖ Read *Leadership Secrets Of Attila The Hun* and Sun Tzu's *The Art of War*.

63 ❖ Negotiate only "win-win" deals.

64 ❖ Make friends with one good lawyer, one
good accountant and one good shrink.

65 ❖ Look for a golden parachute at the end of
your career rainbow.

66 ❖ There's always a silver lining. Find it.

67 ❖ Watch *It's a Wonderful Life* every year.

68 ❖ Talk to people in the elevator.

69 ❖ You get the best results leading by
example, not intimidation.

70 ❖ Don't be stingy with praise, people respond
to it five times faster than criticism.

71 ❖ Mean the compliments you give. Insincere
compliments will backfire.

72 ❖ Respect people's time.

73 ❖ Sweeten criticism with a positive statement first.

74 ❖ Never waffle or beat around the bush when talking about bad financial news.

75 ❖ Delegate the power to improve.

76 ❖ Think a conflict through from the other
person's point of view.

77 ❖ Always allow ample time for preparation.

78 ❖ Rehearse important conversations.

79 ❖ Develop a method that enables you to remember people's names.

80 ❖ Remember the names of associates' and co-workers' spouses and children.

81 ❖ Remember the names of the assistants to the people you deal with—and use them.

82 ❖ Treat the boss's assistant as a significant person.

83 ❖ Send birthday cards to business associates.

84 ❖ After asking a question,
listen to the answer.

85 ❖ Have strong interests outside the office for
a well-rounded life.

86 ❖ Never put work before your family.

87 ❖ Return all phone calls—promptly.

88 ❖ Even the unpleasant ones.

89 ❖ Use upgrades for business travel.

90 ❖ Fly first class when possible and make a
new friend there.

91 ❖ Never complain.

92 ❖ Never make a threat. Reason with people.

93 ❖ Never say never.

94 ❖ Try not to become a person of success,
but rather a person of value.

95 ❖ See situations as they are, not as you wish
them to be—and act on them.

96 ❖ Carefully check every letter you send out
for punctuation, spelling and grammar.

97 ❖ Consider yourself a committee of one.

98 ❖ The bigger the crisis,
the bigger the opportunity.

99 ❖ Those who work hard, play hard.

100 ❖ If you begin too many things,
  you will finish few.

101 ❖ The race is won by running.

102 ❖ If you can fool all of the people some of
     the time, quit while you're ahead.

103 ❖ Mistakes increase experience.
     Experience decreases mistakes.

104 ❖ "Genius is ninety percent per-
spiration and ten percent inspiration."

—*Thomas Edison*

105 ❖ There is only one chance to make a good
first impression.

106 ❖ Don't spend your gross salary.

107 ❖ A job worth doing is worth doing well.

108 ❖ Taking the time to do it right beats
taking the time to do it over.

109 ❖ A good memo is written to either protect
its author or aid others in their tasks. A
great memo does both.

110 ❖ Success is a journey, not a destination.

111 ❖ Call home once a day.

112 ❖ Don't lie—it takes too much effort to keep it going.

113 ❖ Don't cheat—you'll always be looking over your shoulder.

114 ❖ Don't steal—you'll go to jail.

115 ❖ Labels are often fables.

116 ❖ Don't say yes or no until they're finished talking.

117 ❖ The only failure is in no longer trying.

118 ❖ Keep a pad and pencil by your bedside, in the bathroom and in the car.

119 ❖ Good advice is priceless. If not followed, it's worthless.

120 ❖ Just do it!

121 ❖ "No" is a complete sentence.

122 ❖ Recognize when "no" means "yes."

123 ❖ If you need a lot of signposts,
     you may not have a clear destination.

124 ❖ Don't try to tell everything you know.
It may take too short a time.

125 ❖ When you get over-busy,
make an appointment with yourself.

126 ❖ "Don't copy something you can't imitate."—*Yogi Berra*

127 ❖ Money is only a way to keep score.

128 ❖ Don't be early or late. Be on time.

129 ❖ The business of life is not business, but living.

130 ❖ Bureaucracies are there to be outwitted.

131 ❖ Never stop questioning.

132 ❖ Nothing is easy.

133 ❖ Let the other guy win something.

134 ❖ Smile when you're on the phone.

135 ❖ A longer title does not necessarily mean
a more important job.

136 ❖ Accentuate the positive.

137 ❖ To really know someone's character,
    give that person authority.

138 ❖ Responsibility is the greatest incentive.

139 ❖ Incompetence knows no barriers of time
    or place.

140 ❖ Try not to be a plaintiff or a defendant.

141 ❖ Loyalty is worth more than money.

142 ❖ Don't ask for perks or prestige when what
you really want is a raise.

143 ❖ "In a hierarchy, every employee tends to rise to his/her level of incompetence."—The Peter Principle

144 ❖ Read and remember the Golden Rules.

145 ❖ Rest, but never quit when you're behind.

146 ❖ Remember, races are won in the last
few inches.

147 ❖ Overpay someone who is worth it.

148 ❖ Having an idea is one thing.
Making it work is the important part.

149 ❖ Know somebody in Washington.

150 ❖ Take the blame, share the praise.

151 ❖ Work people's strengths.

152 ❖ Experts shouldn't think—
     they should know.

153 ❖ Recognize an expert as one who knows
     more and more about less and less.

154 ❖ Write down your own job description.

155 ❖ A mediocre worker is always at his/her best.

156 ❖ Respect your job—it's the only one you've got.

157 ❖ Always have time on your side.

158 ❖ Always write thank-you letters.

159 ❖ Use your clients' products faithfully.

160 ❖ See your clients in person whenever
possible.

161 ❖ He who dies with the most toys...
　　　　is just as dead.

162 ❖ Success has many friends—
　　　　failure is an orphan.

163 ❖ Time lost is retrievable.
　　　　Time wasted is eternal.

164 ❖ "Let us never negotiate out of fear, but let us never fear to negotiate."

—*John F. Kennedy*

165 ❖ Change is good. Welcome it.

166 ❖ An apology when appropriate is golden.

167 ❖What can go wrong will go wrong.

—Murphy's Law

168 ❖ Asking stupid questions is your right—
just don't abuse the privilege.

169 ❖ It's better to keep your mouth shut at the
risk of people thinking you're dumb, than
to open it and remove all doubt.

170 ❖ The way out of an executive problem is
never as simple as the way in.

171 ❖ Talent is what you possess.

172 ❖ Genius possesses you.

173 ❖ Create something new today.

174 ❖ Life, love and friendship are
the greatest assets.

175 ❖ You are the CEO of your own life.

176 ❖ Riches tend to enlarge rather than
satisfy appetites.

177 ❖ Learn about the new technologies.

178 ❖ "If facts conflict with theory,
either change the theory or the
facts."—*Spinoza*

179 ❖ Dress successfully every day.

180 ❖ Recycle something today.

181 ❖ Write a letter to someone you care about.

182 ❖ Don't mix the bedroom with
the boardroom.

183 ❖ Indecision is the step-sister of flexibility.

184 ❖ Indecision can be fatal.

185 ❖ Avoid reading irrelevant information.

186 ❖ Always cut to the chase.

187 ❖ If you feel you're underpaid,
    find a way to prove it.

188 ❖ Always try again.

189 ❖ Never say:

I thought it was mailed.

I haven't gotten around to it.

I'm waiting for an OK.

190 ❖ Large bureaucracies tend to grow little ones.

191 ❖ A company is known by the people it employs.

192 ❖ Set goals.

193 ❖ The impossible oftentimes isn't.

194 ❖ Never be afraid of contacting
someone "unreachable."

195 ❖ Stay focused.

196 ❖ Get to know the maitre d' at your
favorite restaurant.

197 ❖ Write out a daily game plan every day.

198 ❖ Success has made failures of many.

199 ❖ Don't overreach unnecessarily.

200 ❖ Celebrate victories.

201 ❖ In business as in chess,
   think eight steps ahead.

202 ❖ Think positive.

203 ❖ Above all, THINK!

204 ❖ Humility wears better than hubris.

205 ❖ Always have a fallback position.

206 ❖ Be patient. Whole mountains can be
moved one spoonful at a time.

207 ❖ Read the *Wall St. Journal* whenever
possible.

208 ❖ Setbacks are a part of every business.
Get up, dust yourself off and get back in
the game.

209 ❖ Every employee has an important job.

210 ❖ Don't sweat the small stuff.
It's *all* small stuff.

211 ❖ No bees—no honey. No work—no money.

212 ❖ It's always easier to find a new job
while you're still employed.

213 ❖ Never leave mad.

214 ❖ Listen to your intuition.

215 ❖ Learn from the past, plan for the future,
but live for today.

216 ❖ Learn to laugh at yourself.

217 ❖ Buy into a college fund for your children.

218 ❖ Join community organizations.

219 ❖ Knowledge is power.

220 ❖ Success is never final…failure never fatal.

221 ❖ Recognize extra effort in co-workers.

222 ❖ Act—don't react.

223 ❖ When saying no, be courteous.

224 ❖ Appreciate that the other person is just doing their job.

225 ❖ Avoid confrontations, but don't run from them.

226 ❖ It's dangerous to climb a broken
corporate ladder.

227 ❖ Return more favors than you ask for.

228 ❖ "Anything you can imagine
you can make real."

—*Jules Verne*

229 ❖ Remember that you are not your job.

230 ❖ Make sure the solution is not the chief
cause of more problems.

231 ❖ Don't believe your press clippings.

232 ❖ Create more time with
time-saving devices.

233 ❖ When in doubt, follow your own
moral compass.

234 ❖ Great hopes make greatness.

235 ❖ Wealth is worth less without wisdom.

236 ❖ Tomorrow is always a new day.

237 ❖ Don't talk negatively about
your colleagues.

238 ❖ Equality in all aspects should be based on
ability—not age, race or gender.

239 ❖ A foolish thing said by many is still
a foolish thing.

240 ❖ If you're not going forward,
you're going backward.

241 ❖ Try not to say:

We need approval.

You have to fill out these forms.

Sorry, we've never done it that way before.

But somebody else has tried it.

242 ❖ The creative mind spots wrong questions.

243 ❖ The uncreative mind spots wrong answers.

244 ❖ "Order and simplification are
the first steps toward mastering
a subject."—*Thomas Mann*

245 ❖ Never burn bridges.

246 ❖ In the corporate jungle, make sure
the vine you're swinging on is secure.

247 ❖ Believe in what you're doing.

248 ❖ Be in charge of your own reputation.

249 ❖ Believe that little miracles can happen
every day.

250 ❖ Bring your children to work at least twice a year.

251 ❖ Always try to answer your own questions before asking.

252 ❖ Keep a brief diary of each working day.

253 ❖ Accumulate frequent flyer miles on
at least one major airline.

254 ❖ Success is failure turned inside out.

255 ❖ Sometimes it's better to be lucky
than smart.

256 ❖ Luck is when opportunity
meets preparation.

257 ❖ Contribute to at least one
charity regularly.

258 ❖ Inspire emulation.

259 ❖ Stay within your area of competence,
except when seeking solutions.

260 ❖ Don't keep selling after you get the order.

261 ❖ Cloudy financial mornings often turn
    into clear afternoons.

262 ❖ Call your office and see how long
    it takes to get through.

263 ❖ Read everything you can on
    business ethics.

264 ❖ Nothing replaces persistence.

265 ❖ Know thine enemy.

266 ❖ Slay your enemies with kindness.

267 ❖ Don't take that vacation if you
        didn't finish your work.

268 ❖ Sleep on it before making
monumental decisions.

269 ❖ Bureaucracies defend the status quo long
after the quo has lost its status.

270 ❖ The best way to escape a problem is
to solve it.

271 ❖ Give protéges questions to ask and
answers to remember.

272 ❖ In competitive negotiations, don't reduce
the other side's stress until it's over.

273 ❖ Never respond in anger.
Wait 24 hours to cool off.

274 ❖ Always, always do your best.

275 ❖ Learn something new every day
and pass it on.

276 ❖ Think of what you would change if you
were starting your job tomorrow as a new
employee.

277 ❖ Time is money—overtime is more money.

278 ❖ "Sometimes ya gotta open up
the hood of the car and see
what's wrong."—*Ross Perot*

279 ❖ Make sure your "15 minutes" is for
being famous, not infamous.

280 ❖ The best way is most often the simplest.

281 ❖ A committee keeps minutes
but wastes hours.

282 ❖ The right actions follow correct thoughts.

283 ❖ Review your P and L forecasts
every month.

284 ❖ Don't buy into the collective wisdom
if it's wrong.

285 ❖ After a three-hour lunch, don't return
to the office empty-handed.

286 ❖ "A verbal contract is not worth the paper it's written on."

—*Samuel Goldwyn*

287 ❖ Envy can be fatal.

288 ❖ Ask yourself—
   "What was the original objective?"

289 ❖ Write and send out at least one article
   a year for publication.

290 ❖ Enthusiasm and loyalty are
the best job qualifications.

291 ❖ Retire when it's time.

292 ❖ Always calculate your chances as 50/50.
Either something will happen or it won't.

293 ❖ Respect subordinates and
they will respect you.

294 ❖ Like subordinates and they will like you.

295 ❖ Ridicule subordinates and
they will ridicule you.

296 ❖ Berate subordinates and they will
turn on you.

297 ❖ Follow that most difficult
principle—Buy low, sell high.

298 ❖ Know the answer to these questions:

Where am I?

Where do I want to be?

Where do I want to be in 5 years?

How am I getting there?

How will I know I'm there?

299 ❖ Teach your child's class something
you know.

300 ❖ Listen to advice graciously.

301 ❖ Catch an employee doing something good.

302 ❖ Give people a chance.

303 ❖ The higher the level, the clearer the air.
The clearer the air, the better the view.

304 ❖ When you want something,
always ask the person on top.

305 ❖ Remember that a 1000 mile journey
begins with a single step.

306 ❖ Don't act on past fears.

307 ❖ Keep a dictionary and thesaurus on
your desk—and use them!

308 ❖ If you don't know—say so. Then find out.

309 ❖ If you drink alcoholic beverages at
business meals, order by brand name.

310 ❖ The longer the letter, the less chance
it will be read.

311 ❖ Take a fresh look at last year's organiza-
tional charts and department manuals.

312 ❖ Ask the mailboy, the receptionist and the
newest employee what they think of the
company.

313 ❖ If your company has season tickets to
something, use them.

314 ❖ Sit by yourself and listen to
Madame Butterfly.

315 ❖ Master yourself. Only then can you
master others.

316 ❖ Remember—advice, when most needed,
   is least heeded.

317 ❖ Problems are organic. Deal with them
   immediately or they'll grow.

318 ❖ Don't crawl out on a limb for someone
   holding a saw.

319 ❖ Don't criticize anyone publicly.

320 ❖ "If you can't stand the heat, get
out of the kitchen."—*Harry S Truman*

321 ❖ He who knows nothing, doubts nothing.

322 ❖ Negotiate with confidence, not arrogance.

323 ❖ Imagine who you would like to be
when you grow up.

324 ❖ Be rational, not impulsive.

325 ❖ Don't let anyone rush you.

326 ❖ Understand that you must
control your own destiny.

327 ❖ Lead with your head, follow with
    your heart.

328 ❖ Read Al Gore's *Earth In The Balance*.

329 ❖ Success is the child of audacity.

330 ❖ A little knowledge is dangerous.

331 ❖ Always search for a better way.

332 ❖ Structure the negotiation so the other side always has an alternative.

333 ❖ It's not who you know, it's *whom* you know.

334 ❖ In a negotiation, never let the other side
know what you're thinking.

335 ❖ Always have a joke ready.

336 ❖ Always try one more time.

337 ❖ Genius is in the details.

338 ❖ Admit when you're wrong.

339 ❖ Don't be afraid to admit you
don't understand.

340 ❖ Learn to project an impressive image.

341 ❖ Communication is everything.

342 ❖ Stumbling blocks are stepping stones
in disguise.

343 ❖ "Only those who dare to fail greatly can ever achieve greatly."

—*Robert F. Kennedy*

344 ❖ Believe that where there's a will,
      there's a way.

345 ❖ Strive to enhance the quality of your life
      at work and at home.

346 ❖ Make things happen the way you
      want them to.

347 ❖ Never hesitate to cut losses.

348 ❖ Always have a collateral objective.

349 ❖ If you need someone's help,
    come right out and ask for it.

350 ❖ Don't define yourself too narrowly.

351 ❖ Reward loyalty.

352 ❖ Try not to say:

It's not for us.

We have it on file somewhere.

We'll keep it under advisement.

We'll get back to you.

353 ❖ Choose an occupation that is as
satisfying personally as it is financially.

354 ❖ Ask for input.

355 ❖ Choose good people.

356 ❖ "The person who figures out how to harness the collective genius of the people in his/her organization is going to blow the competition away."

—*Walter Wriston*, Harvard Business Review

357 ❖ Shop around.

358 ❖ Take good notes.

359 ❖ Some people make excuses.
   The others make progress.

360 ❖ Cultivate the ability to stand up
   under punishment.

361 ❖ Learn self-reliance.

362 ❖ Never fear failure.

363 ❖ Enthusiasm is contagious.

364 ❖ Never say:

It's not my job.

It's not my department.

That's the way it's done here.

365 ❖ The only true success is to be able to live your life your own way.

Favorites

   1.

   2.

   3.

4.

5.

6.